CW01426309

EASY LO
COOKBOOK

THE EFFORTLESS CHEF SERIES

By
Chef Maggie Chow

Published by
BookSumo, a division of Saxonberg
Associates
http://www.booksumo.com/

STAY TO THE END OF THE COOKBOOK AND RECEIVE....

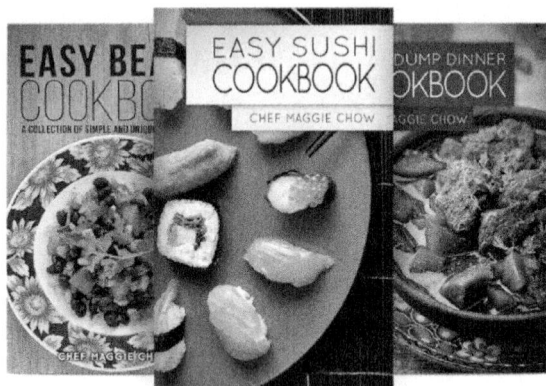

I really appreciate when people, take the time to read all of my recipes.

So, as a gift for reading this entire cookbook you will receive a **massive collection of special recipes.**

Read to the end of and get my *Easy Specialty Cookbook Box Set for FREE*!

This box set includes the following:

1. *Easy Sushi Cookbook*

2. **Easy Dump Dinner Cookbook**
3. **Easy Beans Cookbook**

Remember this box set is about **EASY** cooking.

In the **Easy Sushi Cookbook** you will learn the easiest methods to prepare almost every type of Japanese Sushi i.e. *California Rolls, the Perfect Sushi Rice, Crab Rolls, Osaka Style Sushi*, and so many others.

Then we go on to *Dump Dinners*. Nothing can be easier than a Dump Dinner. In the **Easy Dump Dinner Cookbook** we will learn how to master our slow cookers and make some amazingly unique dinners that will take almost **no effort**.

Finally in the **Easy Beans Cookbook** we tackle one of my favorite side dishes: Beans. There are so many delicious ways to make Baked Beans and Bean Salads that I had to share them.

So stay till the end and then keep on cooking with my *Easy Specialty Cookbook Box Set*!

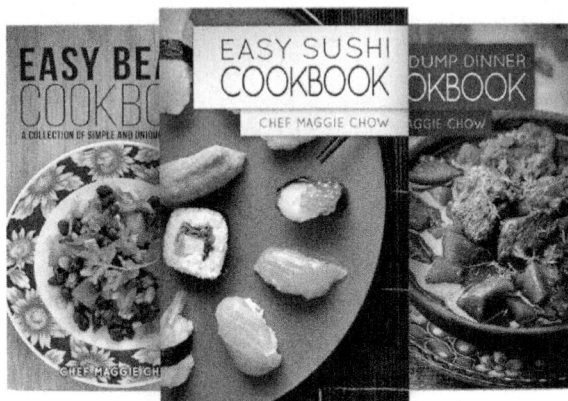

ABOUT THE AUTHOR.

Maggie Chow is the author and creator of your favorite *Easy Cookbooks* and *The Effortless Chef Series*. Maggie is a lover of all things related to food. Maggie loves nothing more than finding new recipes, trying them out, and then making them her own, by adding or removing ingredients, tweaking cooking times, and anything to make the recipe not only taste better, but be easier to cook!

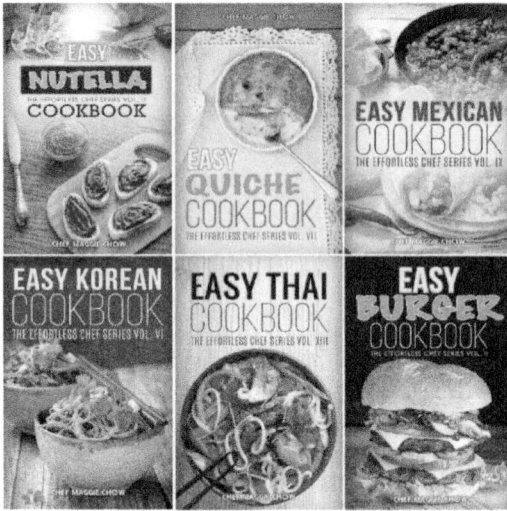

For a complete listing of all my books please see my author page.

INTRODUCTION

Welcome to *The Effortless Chef Series*! Thank you for taking the time to download the *Easy Louisiana Cookbook*. Come take a journey with me into the delights of easy cooking. The point of this cookbook and all my cookbooks is to exemplify the effortless nature of cooking simply.

In this book we focus on food from Louisiana. You will find that even though the recipes are simple, the taste of the dishes is quite amazing.

So will you join me in an adventure of simple cooking? If the answer is yes (and I hope it is) please consult the table of contents to find the dishes you are most interested in. Once you are ready jump right in and start cooking.

— Chef Maggie Chow

TABLE OF CONTENTS

ANY ISSUES? CONTACT ME

If you find that something important to you is missing from this book please contact me at maggie@booksumo.com.

I will try my best to re-publish a revised copy taking your feedback into consideration and let you know when the book has been revised with you in mind.

:)

— Chef Maggie Chow

LEGAL NOTES

COMMON ABBREVIATIONS

cup(s)	C.
tablespoon	tbsp
teaspoon	tsp
ounce	oz.
pound	lb

*All units used are standard American measurements

Chapter 1: Easy Louisiana Recipes

Rice and Beans

Ingredients

- 1 lb dry kidney beans
- 1/4 C. olive oil
- 1 large onion, chopped
- 1 green bell pepper, chopped
- 2 tbsps minced garlic
- 2 stalks celery, chopped
- 6 C. water
- 2 bay leaves
- 1/2 tsp cayenne pepper
- 1 tsp dried thyme
- 1/4 tsp dried sage
- 1 tbsp dried parsley
- 1 tsp Cajun seasoning
- 1 lb andouille sausage, sliced
- 4 C. water

- 2 C. long grain white rice

Directions

- Get a bowl and fill it with water. Leave your beans submerged in the water for at least 8 hrs or throughout the night.
- For 6 mins fry in olive oil: celery, onions, garlic, and bell peppers.
- Add 6 C. of water to a saucepan and then transfer your beans to it after rinsing them.
- Combine in your onions, peppers, and the following: Cajun seasoning, bay leaves, parsley, cayenne, sage, and thyme.
- Get the mix boiling then set the heat to low and let the mix lightly cook for 2 h 40 m.
- Now combine in your sausage and let everything continue cooking for 35 more mins.
- Get a 2nd saucepan and bring some water to a boil. Enter in

your rice, place a lid on the pot, and let the rice cook for 22 mins.

- Enjoy your rice with the beans.

Amount per serving (8 total)

Timing Information:

Preparation	25 m
Cooking	3 h 5 m
Total Time	11 h 30 m

Nutritional Information:

Calories	630 kcal
Fat	24.2 g
Carbohydrates	79.1g
Protein	24 g
Cholesterol	33 mg
Sodium	604 mg

* Percent Daily Values are based on a 2,000 calorie diet.

ETOUFFEE

Ingredients

- 3 C. long grain white rice
- 6 C. water
- 3/4 C. butter
- 1 large onion, chopped
- 1 clove garlic, chopped
- 1/4 C. all-purpose flour
- 1 lb crawfish tails
- 2 tbsps canned tomato sauce
- 1 C. water, or as needed
- 6 green onions, chopped
- salt and pepper to taste
- 1 1/2 tbsps Cajun seasoning, or to taste

Directions

- Boil your water in a large pot then add your rice.

- Place a lid on the pot, set the heat to its lowest level and lightly boil for 22 mins.
- Stir fry your onions in butter until they are see-through and then add your garlic.
- Continue stirring for 2 mins then add the flour to the onions and stir for a few more mins.
- Then add the crawfish, water, and tomato sauce. Get everything simmering and then add your salt, Cajun seasoning, green onions, and pepper.
- Let everything simmer for about 12 to 15 mins with a low level of heat.
- Enjoy your fish over the rice.

Amount per serving (6 total)

Timing Information:

Preparation	15 m
Cooking	15 m
Total Time	30 m

Nutritional Information:

Calories	636 kcal
Fat	24.6 g
Carbohydrates	82.7g
Protein	19.4 g
Cholesterol	142 mg
Sodium	601 mg

* Percent Daily Values are based on a 2,000 calorie diet.

Easy Chicken Fry

Ingredients

- 1 (3 lb) whole chicken, cut into 6 pieces
- 2 eggs, beaten
- 1 (12 fluid oz.) can evaporated milk
- 2 tsps salt
- 2 tsps ground black pepper
- 2 tsps garlic powder
- 2 tsps onion powder
- 2 1/2 C. all-purpose flour
- 1 1/2 C. vegetable oil for frying

Directions

- Get a bowl mix: milk, onion powder, eggs, garlic powder, pepper, and salt.
- Get a 2nd bowl and add the flour to it.

- Coat the chicken first with the wet mix and then the dry flour.
- Now fry your chicken in hot oil for about 7 to 10 mins per side until it is fully done.
- Enjoy.

Amount per serving (6 total)

Timing Information:

Preparation	10 m
Cooking	20 m
Total Time	30 m

Nutritional Information:

Calories	638 kcal
Fat	29.6 g
Carbohydrates	47.9g
Protein	42.7 g
Cholesterol	177 mg
Sodium	960 mg

* Percent Daily Values are based on a 2,000 calorie diet.

SHRIMP BAKE

Ingredients

- 1 1/2 C. uncooked instant rice
- 1 1/2 C. water
- 1 tsp vegetable oil
- 1 lb small shrimp, peeled and deveined
- 2 tbsps butter
- 1 (4 oz.) can sliced mushrooms, drained
- 1 (10.75 oz.) can condensed cream of shrimp soup
- 1 (8 oz.) container sour cream
- 3/4 C. shredded Cheddar cheese

Directions

- Coat a casserole dish with oil and then turn on the broiler to low, if possible, before doing anything else.

- Get a saucepan and boil your water.
- Then enter your rice into and it and place a lid on the pot.
- Set the heat to low and let the rice cook for 12 mins. Now shut off the heat.
- Stir fry your shrimp for 4 mins, in oil, then place them in a bowl.
- In the same pot add some butter and fry your mushrooms for 3 mins then add in your sour cream and soup.
- Get the soup hot but avoid boiling it.
- Now add the shrimp back to the pan and heat it up.
- Put everything in your casserole dish including the rice.
- Garnish the casserole with some cheese and cook everything under the broiler for 5 mins.
- Enjoy.

Amount per serving (4 total)

Timing Information:

Preparation	15 m
Cooking	25 m
Total Time	40 m

Nutritional Information:

Calories	572 kcal
Fat	31.9 g
Carbohydrates	38.5g
Protein	31.8 g
Cholesterol	250 mg
Sodium	1150 mg

* Percent Daily Values are based on a 2,000 calorie diet.

NEW ORLEANS STYLE PANCAKES

Ingredients

- 3/4 lb sweet potatoes
- 1 1/2 C. all-purpose flour
- 3 1/2 tsps baking powder
- 1 tsp salt
- 1/2 tsp ground nutmeg
- 2 eggs, beaten
- 1 1/2 C. milk
- 1/4 C. butter, melted

Directions

- For 17 mins boil your sweet potatoes in water.
- Dump these potatoes in a bowl of cold water immediately after boiling them. Then remove all the skins, chunk them, and mash them.

- Get a bowl, sift: nutmeg, flour, salt, and baking powder.
- Get a 2nd bowl, combine: butter, potatoes, milk, and eggs.
- Heat up a frying pan or a griddle that has been oiled or coated with nonstick spray.
- Now combine both bowls to form a batter.
- Fry tbsps of this mixture until you find one side begins to form bubbles, then flip the pancake and cook it for the same amount of time.
- The cooking time is very dependent upon the heat of stove.
- Enjoy.

Amount per serving (8 total)

Timing Information:

Preparation	10 m
Cooking	15 m
Total Time	45 m

Nutritional Information:

Calories	215 kcal
Fat	8.2 g
Carbohydrates	29.2g
Protein	6.2 g
Cholesterol	65 mg
Sodium	549 mg

* Percent Daily Values are based on a 2,000 calorie diet.

GUMBO I

Ingredients

- 1 (3 lb) whole chicken
- 1/2 C. all-purpose flour
- 1/2 C. vegetable oil
- 1 (10 oz.) package frozen chopped onions
- 1 (10 oz.) package frozen green bell peppers
- 5 stalks celery, finely chopped
- 1 tbsp Cajun seasoning (such as Tony Chachere's), or to taste
- 2 whole bay leaves
- 1 (28 oz.) can diced tomatoes
- 1 lb fully-cooked smoked beef sausage (such as Hillshire Farm(R)), sliced
- 1 (10 oz.) package frozen sliced okra
- salt and black pepper to taste

Directions

- Boil your water and salt, then simmer your chicken in it for 1 hour until fully cooked.
- Take the chicken out from the water and cut it in half to cool faster.
- Keep the water the chicken was cooked in.
- Once the chicken is no longer hot take off the meat from the bones.
- Now get a big pan and mix: veggie oil and flour together to form a roux.
- Make this roux with a low level of heat and constantly stir it for about 22 mins until it becomes brown.
- Once it is brown add in: bay leaves, onions, Cajun seasoning, celery and bell peppers.
- Again with a low heat let the veggies simmer for 40 mins.
- Now add the chicken broth (the boiled water), sausage, and diced tomatoes.
- Let the contents simmer for 1 more hour.

- Now add in your meat from the chicken and your okra and let everything simmer for 50 more mins.
- Enjoy your gumbo.

Amount per serving (10 total)

Timing Information:

Preparation	20 m
Cooking	3 h 15 m
Total Time	3 h 55 m

Nutritional Information:

Calories	437 kcal
Fat	32.2 g
Carbohydrates	14.5g
Protein	21.4 g
Cholesterol	67 mg
Sodium	873 mg

* Percent Daily Values are based on a
2,000 calorie diet.

A Stew from Louisiana

Ingredients

- 2 tbsps all-purpose flour
- 1 tsp salt
- 1/2 tsp celery salt
- 1/4 tsp garlic salt
- 1/4 tsp black pepper
- 1/2 tsp ground ginger
- 3 lbs chuck roast, cut into 2-inch pieces
- 2 tbsps bacon drippings
- 1 (14.5 oz.) can diced tomatoes
- 3 medium onions, chopped
- 1/3 C. red wine vinegar
- 1/2 C. molasses
- 1/2 C. water
- 6 carrots, chopped
- 1/2 C. raisins
- 4 C. cooked rice

Directions

- Get a bowl, mix evenly: ground ginger, flour, black pepper, garlic salt, regular salt, and celery salt.
- Coat your meat with this seasoning.
- Stir fry this meat in bacon fat until all sides are nice and brown.
- Now combine in: water, diced tomatoes, molasses, onions, and vinegar. Place a lid on your pot and let the contents lightly boil with a low heat for 2 hrs.
- Now finally add in your raisins and carrots and simmer for 35 more mins.
- Enjoy with jasmine or your favorite rice.

Amount per serving (8 total)

Timing Information:

Preparation	15 m
Cooking	2 h 30 m
Total Time	2 h 45 m

Nutritional Information:

Calories	531 kcal
Fat	22.6 g
Carbohydrates	57g
Protein	23.9 g
Cholesterol	81 mg
Sodium	616 mg

* Percent Daily Values are based on a 2,000 calorie diet.

SWEET BANANA STIR FRY

Ingredients

- 1/4 C. butter
- 2/3 C. dark brown sugar
- 3 1/2 tbsps rum
- 1 1/2 tsps vanilla extract
- 1/2 tsp ground cinnamon
- 3 bananas, peeled and sliced lengthwise and crosswise
- 1/4 C. coarsely chopped walnuts
- 1 pint vanilla ice cream

Directions

- Stir fry the following in butter: cinnamon, sugar, vanilla, and rum.
- Once the mix is bubbly add your nuts and bananas.
- Let the contents simmer for 3 mins.
- Enjoy with ice cream.

Amount per serving (4 total)

Timing Information:

Preparation	5 m
Cooking	15 m
Total Time	20 m

Nutritional Information:

Calories	534 kcal
Fat	23.8 g
Carbohydrates	73.2g
Protein	4.6 g
Cholesterol	60 mg
Sodium	146 mg

* Percent Daily Values are based on a 2,000 calorie diet.

Jambalaya I

Ingredients

- 1 lb skinless, boneless chicken breast halves - cut into 1 inch cubes
- 1 lb andouille sausage, sliced
- 1 (28 oz.) can diced tomatoes with juice
- 1 large onion, chopped
- 1 large green bell pepper, chopped
- 1 C. chopped celery
- 1 C. chicken broth
- 2 tsps dried oregano
- 2 tsps dried parsley
- 2 tsps Cajun seasoning
- 1 tsp cayenne pepper
- 1/2 tsp dried thyme
- 1 lb frozen cooked shrimp without tails

Directions

- Cook the following on low for 8 hours in your slow cooker: thyme, chicken, cayenne, sausage, Cajun seasoning, tomatoes and juice, parsley, onions, oregano, bell peppers, broth, and celery.
- Enjoy with rice.

Amount per serving (12 total)

Timing Information:

Preparation	20 m
Cooking	8 h
Total Time	8 h 20 m

Nutritional Information:

Calories	235 kcal
Fat	13.6 g
Carbohydrates	6.1g
Protein	20.2 g
Cholesterol	99 mg
Sodium	688 mg

* Percent Daily Values are based on a 2,000 calorie diet.

GUMBO II

Ingredients

- 1 tbsp olive oil
- 1 C. skinless, boneless chicken breast halves - chopped
- 1/2 lb pork sausage links, thinly sliced
- 1 C. olive oil
- 1 C. all-purpose flour
- 2 tbsps minced garlic
- 3 quarts chicken broth
- 1 (12 fluid oz.) can or bottle beer
- 6 stalks celery, diced
- 4 roma (plum) tomatoes, diced
- 1 sweet onion, sliced
- 1 (10 oz.) can diced tomatoes with green chili peppers, with liquid
- 2 tbsps chopped fresh red chili peppers
- 1 bunch fresh parsley, chopped
- 1/4 C. Cajun seasoning
- 1 lb shrimp, peeled and deveined

Directions

- Stir fry your chicken in hot oil until fully done. Then add in your sausage and continue to stir fry until it is done as well.
- Place the contents in a bowl.
- In the same pan or a new one make a roux with flour and olive oil.
- Once it is brown add your garlic and stir fry the mix for 2 mins.
- Combine the following with your roux while stirring: beer, and broth.
- Get the roux simmering and then add: Cajun seasoning, celery, parsley, tomatoes, red chili peppers, sweet onions, diced tomatoes.
- Let your roux lightly boil with a covering for 45 mins with low heat.
- Stir the roux every 5 to 7 mins.

- Then combine in your sausage and chicken and simmer for 25 more mins.
- Enjoy.

Amount per serving (10 total)

Timing Information:

Preparation	1 h
Cooking	1 h
Total Time	2 h

Nutritional Information:

Calories	419 kcal
Fat	28.7 g
Carbohydrates	17.3g
Protein	20.5 g
Cholesterol	99 mg
Sodium	900 mg

* Percent Daily Values are based on a 2,000 calorie diet.

Jambalaya II

Ingredients

- 2 tbsps peanut oil, divided
- 1 tbsp Cajun seasoning
- 10 oz. andouille sausage, sliced into rounds
- 1 lb boneless skinless chicken breasts, cut into 1 inch pieces
- 1 onion, diced
- 1 small green bell pepper, diced
- 2 stalks celery, diced
- 3 cloves garlic, minced
- 1 (16 oz.) can crushed Italian tomatoes
- 1/2 tsp red pepper flakes
- 1/2 tsp ground black pepper
- 1 tsp salt
- 1/2 tsp hot pepper sauce
- 2 tsps Worcestershire sauce
- 1 tsp file powder
- 1 1/4 C. uncooked white rice
- 2 1/2 C. chicken broth

Directions

- Get a bowl, mix: chicken and sausage with Cajun seasoning.
- Then fry your seasoned meats in 2 tbsps of peanut oil in a Dutch oven until fully browned.
- Now put the meats in a 2nd bowl.
- Add to the same pot: garlic, onions, celery, and bell peppers.
- Stir the contents fry until everything is soft then add: hot sauce, file powder, red pepper, salt, Worcestershire, black pepper, and crushed tomatoes.
- Cook the mix for 5 mins then add your meats and cook everything for 13 more mins.
- Add the broth and the rice.
- Get everything boiling, set the heat to low, and let the contents simmer for 30 mins until all the liquid has evaporated.
- Enjoy.

Amount per serving (6 total)

Timing Information:

Preparation	20 m
Cooking	45 m
Total Time	1 h 5 m

Nutritional Information:

Calories	465 kcal
Fat	19.8 g
Carbohydrates	42.4g
Protein	28.1 g
Cholesterol	73 mg
Sodium	1633 mg

* Percent Daily Values are based on a 2,000 calorie diet.

JAMBALAYA III

Ingredients

- 8 skinless, boneless chicken breast halves - diced
- 6 C. chicken broth
- 3 C. long grain white rice
- 1 lb smoked sausage, sliced
- 1/4 C. vegetable oil
- 1 green bell pepper, seeded and chopped
- 1 small onion, finely chopped
- 4 carrots, thinly sliced
- 2 stalks celery, thinly sliced
- 1 (8 oz.) can mushroom pieces, drained
- 1/4 tsp cayenne pepper, or to taste
- salt and pepper to taste

Directions

- Stir fry your onions until tender, in oil, in a big pot.
- Then combine in your chicken and stir fry it until the chicken is browned evenly.
- Combine in the following with your chicken and onions: sausage, carrots, bell pepper, mushrooms, and celery.
- Cook this mix for 2 mins while stirring.
- Now add your broth and get it boiling.
- Once everything is boiling pour in your pepper, cayenne, salt, and rice.
- Place a lid on the pot, set the heat to a low level, and let the rice simmer for 22 mins.
- At this point all the liquid should have evaporated (if not continue simmering).
- Enjoy.

Amount per serving (12 total)

Timing Information:

Preparation	15 m
Cooking	25 m
Total Time	40 m

Nutritional Information:

Calories	463 kcal
Fat	18.9 g
Carbohydrates	42.2g
Protein	28.8 g
Cholesterol	71 mg
Sodium	711 mg

* Percent Daily Values are based on a 2,000 calorie diet.

CREOLE STYLE CHICKEN BREASTS

Ingredients

- 1/4 lb bacon
- 4 skinless, boneless chicken breast halves - cut into strips
- 1 tsp Cajun seasoning
- 1 tbsp light olive oil
- 1 head romaine lettuce- rinsed, dried and chopped
- 1/2 C. Caesar salad dressing
- 1/3 C. grated Parmesan cheese

Directions

- Fry your bacon. Then break it into pieces and place it in a separate bowl.
- Now add your olive oil, seasonings, and chicken to the same pan.

- Fry the chicken until fully done and brown all over.
- Shut off the heat.
- Once the chicken has a cooled a bit slice it.
- Get a big bowl, combine: bacon, lettuce, parmesan, and salad dressing.
- Stir the salad with two large forks to coat the lettuce evenly with dressing then place the salad on serving dishes.
- On each dish add some chicken pieces.
- Enjoy.

Amount per serving (4 total)

Timing Information:

Preparation	15 m
Cooking	35 m
Total Time	50 m

Nutritional Information:

Calories	376 kcal
Fat	24.7 g
Carbohydrates	4.4g
Protein	32.6 g
Cholesterol	95 mg
Sodium	815 mg

* Percent Daily Values are based on a 2,000 calorie diet.

BOURBON CHICKEN

Ingredients

- 4 skinless, boneless chicken breast halves
- 1 tsp ground ginger
- 4 oz. soy sauce
- 2 tbsps dried minced onion
- 1/2 C. packed brown sugar
- 3/8 C. bourbon
- 1/2 tsp garlic powder

Directions

- Get a bowl, combine: garlic powder, ginger, bourbon, soy sauce, sugar, and onions flakes.
- Layer a casserole dish with the chicken.
- Then coat the chicken with your wet mix.
- Let the casserole sit in the fridge for at least 8 hours or throughout

the night covered with plastic wrap or a lid.
- Now set your oven to 325 degrees before doing anything else.
- Cook the chicken in the oven for 1.5 hours and baste it every 10 to 12 mins.
- Enjoy with rice.

Amount per serving (4 total)

Timing Information:

Preparation	10 m
Cooking	10 h
Total Time	10 h 10 m

Nutritional Information:

Calories	313 kcal
Fat	1.5 g
Carbohydrates	31.2g
Protein	29.3 g
Cholesterol	68 mg
Sodium	1664 mg

* Percent Daily Values are based on a 2,000 calorie diet.

Jambalaya IV

Ingredients

- 3 tbsps all-purpose flour
- 2 tbsps olive oil
- 1 (12 oz.) package chicken apple sausage
- 2 tbsps olive oil
- 3/4 C. chopped onion
- 3/4 C. chopped green bell pepper
- 1 tbsp minced garlic
- 2 bay leaves
- 1 1/2 C. long grain rice
- 1 1/2 tsps dried thyme
- 1/2 tsp salt
- 3/4 tsp chili powder
- 1/2 tsp white pepper
- 1/2 tsp black pepper
- 1/2 tsp red pepper flakes
- 1/3 C. white wine
- 3/4 C. canned crushed tomatoes
- 1 1/2 C. chicken broth
- 3/4 lb peeled and deveined medium shrimp

- 1/2 C. diced fresh pineapple
- 1/2 C. diced mango
- 1/2 C. diced apple

Directions

- Oil a baking dish and set your oven to 400 degrees before doing anything else.
- Fry your sausages in 2 tbsps of olive oil for 3 mins per side after coating them with flour. Then place them to the side for later.
- Stir fry the following until soft in 2 more tbsps of olive oil for 4 mins: bay leans, onions, garlic, and green pepper.
- Now add your rice and stir fry the mix until the rice becomes slightly translucent for 5 mins.
- Now add: black peppers, chicken broth, salt, thyme, tomatoes, chili powder, wine, red pepper flakes, and white pepper.
- Get the tomato mix boiling.

- Once the mix is boiling shut the heat, add in the sausages, put a lid on the pan, and cook everything in the oven for 30 mins.
- Now take out the pot and add: apples, shrimp, mango, and pineapple.
- Stir everything a few times and place it back in the oven for 15 more mins.
- Enjoy.

Amount per serving (6 total)

Timing Information:

Preparation	30 m
Cooking	40 m
Total Time	1 h 10 m

Nutritional Information:

Calories	478 kcal
Fat	15.9 g
Carbohydrates	55g
Protein	24.9 g
Cholesterol	123 mg
Sodium	1074 mg

* Percent Daily Values are based on a 2,000 calorie diet.

ETOUFFE II

Ingredients

- 1/3 C. vegetable oil
- 1/4 C. all-purpose flour
- 1 small green bell pepper, diced
- 1 medium onion, chopped
- 2 cloves garlic, minced
- 2 stalks celery, diced
- 2 fresh tomatoes, chopped
- 2 tbsps Louisiana-style hot sauce
- 1/3 tsp ground cayenne pepper (optional)
- 2 tbsps seafood seasoning
- 1/2 tsp ground black pepper
- 1 C. fish stock
- 1 lb crawfish tails
- 1 lb medium shrimp - peeled and deveined

Directions

- Stir fry flour in a pan for 15 to 22 mins until its color becomes brown.
- Now add your bell peppers, onions, celery, and garlic.
- Cook this for 7 mins until tender.
- Now add the seafood seasoning, fish stock, and tomatoes.
- Set your heat to the lowest level and let the contents lightly boil for 22 mins.
- Stir the mix every 3 mins.
- Finally add in some cayenne and hot sauce and finally your shrimp and crawfish.
- Let the fish simmer in the sauce 13 mins.
- Enjoy.

Amount per serving (6 total)

Timing Information:

Preparation	20 m
Cooking	50 m
Total Time	1 h 10 m

Nutritional Information:

Calories	264 kcal
Fat	14 g
Carbohydrates	9g
Protein	24.9 g
Cholesterol	196 mg
Sodium	956 mg

* Percent Daily Values are based on a
2,000 calorie diet.

CREOLE ANGEL HAIR

Ingredients

- 1 (8 oz.) package angel hair pasta
- 1/4 C. butter
- 1 lb shrimp, peeled and deveined
- 1 clove garlic, minced
- 1/4 C. all-purpose flour
- 2 tbsps Cajun seasoning
- 2 C. milk
- 1/4 tsp salt
- 1 tbsp lemon juice

Directions

- Boil your pasta in water and salt for 7 mins.
- Stir fry your shrimp for 3 mins in melted butter.
- Then add in your garlic and cook everything for 3 more mins.

- Take everything out of the pan and add in the Cajun seasoning and flour.
- Stir the contents while heating for 7 mins.
- Slowly add the milk and keep heating it until everything becomes thick.
- Once your seasoned milk is thick shut off the heat and add in your shrimp and garlic.
- Add your preferred amount of salt and also some lemon juice, but add the lemon juice first.
- Ladle Cajun sauce over pasta and enjoy.

Amount per serving (4 total)

Timing Information:

Preparation	10 m
Cooking	10 m
Total Time	20 m

Nutritional Information:

Calories	483 kcal
Fat	17.6 g
Carbohydrates	46g
Protein	34.4 g
Cholesterol	213 mg
Sodium	1271 mg

* Percent Daily Values are based on a 2,000 calorie diet.

Cajun Gumbo IV

Ingredients

- 1 C. vegetable oil
- 1 C. all-purpose flour
- 1 large onion, chopped
- 1 large green bell pepper, chopped
- 2 celery stalks, chopped
- 1 lb andouille or smoked sausage, sliced 1/4 inch thick
- 4 cloves garlic, minced
- salt and pepper to taste
- Creole seasoning to taste
- 6 C. chicken broth
- 1 bay leaf
- 1 rotisserie chicken, boned and shredded

Directions

- For 12 mins stir fry flour and oil to make a brown roux.

- But make sure your roux does not have any black dots in it.
- If so, try again.
- Now add the: sausage, onions, celery, and bell peppers.
- Cook this mix for 7 mins.
- Add in your garlic and let the contents cook for 6 more mins.
- Add: creole seasoning, pepper, broth, salt, and bay leaf.
- Get this all boiling and then set the heat to low and let the mix lightly cook for 1 hour.
- Finally add in your chicken and cook the contents for 1 more hour.
- Stir the mix every 10 mins.
- Enjoy.

Amount per serving (10 total)

Timing Information:

Preparation	45 m
Cooking	2 h 30 m
Total Time	3 h 15 m

Nutritional Information:

Calories	478 kcal
Fat	39.4 g
Carbohydrates	14.3g
Protein	16 g
Cholesterol	56 mg
Sodium	1045 mg

* Percent Daily Values are based on a 2,000 calorie diet.

CREOLE SHRIMP

Ingredients

- 1/2 C. finely diced onion
- 1/2 C. chopped green bell pepper
- 1/2 C. chopped celery
- 2 cloves garlic, minced
- 3 tbsps butter
- 2 tbsps cornstarch
- 1 (14.5 oz.) can stewed tomatoes
- 1 (8 oz.) can tomato sauce
- 1 tbsp Worcestershire sauce
- 1 tsp chili powder
- 1 dash hot pepper sauce
- 1 lb medium shrimp - peeled and deveined

Directions

- Fry your garlic, onions, celery, and green peppers until soft. Then add in your cornstarch, red

pepper sauce, all the tomatoes, chili powder, and Worcestershire.
- Get the contents boiling then add in your shrimp.
- Cook the shrimp while stirring for 7 mins.
- Enjoy with rice.

Amount per serving (5 total)

Timing Information:

Preparation	20 m
Cooking	25 m
Total Time	45 m

Nutritional Information:

Calories	193 kcal
Fat	8.1 g
Carbohydrates	14.3g
Protein	16.8 g
Cholesterol	157 mg
Sodium	677 mg

* Percent Daily Values are based on a 2,000 calorie diet.

Northeast Louisiana Style Cajun Wings with Sweet and Spicy Sauce

Ingredients

- 6 lbs chicken wings, separated at joints, tips discarded
- 1 1/2 C. Louisiana-style hot sauce
- 3/4 C. butter
- 1 C. honey
- 1 pinch garlic salt
- 1 pinch ground black pepper
- 1 tsp cayenne pepper, or to taste
- 1 tsp red pepper flakes

Directions

- You will need a grill for this recipe. So heat yours up after oiling the grate.
- Cook the chicken on the grill for 10 mins per side until fully done.

- Then place the chicken in a saucepan.
- In a 2nd saucepan boil the following for 12 mins: cayenne, hot sauce, black pepper, butter, garlic salt, and honey.
- Cover your wings in this wet sauce and finally sprinkle on the pepper flakes.
- Enjoy.

NOTE: Instead of using a grill, which is preferred you can fry then, bake these wings for a good taste as well. Fry the chicken first, then coat it with the sauce by tossing the wings in a bowl. Then bake them for a bit in the oven until crispy.

Amount per serving (12 total)

Timing Information:

Preparation	15 m
Cooking	30 m
Total Time	45 m

Nutritional Information:

Calories	356 kcal
Fat	22.7 g
Carbohydrates	23.9g
Protein	15.6 g
Cholesterol	78 mg
Sodium	896 mg

* Percent Daily Values are based on a
2,000 calorie diet.

Muffuletta

(Louisiana Sandwhich)

Ingredients

- 1 C. pimento-stuffed green olives, crushed
- 1/2 C. drained kalamata olives, crushed
- 2 cloves garlic, minced
- 1/4 C. roughly chopped pickled cauliflower florets
- 2 tbsps drained capers
- 1 tbsp chopped celery
- 1 tbsp chopped carrot
- 1/2 C. pepperoncini, drained
- 1/4 C. marinated cocktail onions
- 1/2 tsp celery seed
- 1 tsp dried oregano
- 1 tsp dried basil
- 3/4 tsp ground black pepper
- 1/4 C. red wine vinegar
- 1/2 C. olive oil
- 1/4 C. canola oil

- 2 (1 lb) loaves Italian bread
- 8 oz. thinly sliced Genoa salami
- 8 oz. thinly sliced cooked ham
- 8 oz. sliced mortadella
- 8 oz. sliced mozzarella cheese
- 8 oz. sliced provolone cheese

Directions

- Get a bowl, combine: all oils, all your olives, vinegar, garlic, black pepper, cauliflower, basil, capers, oregano, celery, celery seed, carrot, pepperoncini, and cocktail onions.
- Let the salad sit covered in the fridge for at least 6 to 8 hours.
- Dice your bread into two pieces horizontally.
- Remove some the insides of the bread to make more space.
- Top each piece with some salad.
- On the bottom part of your bread layer: cheese, salami, mortadella, and ham.

- Form your sandwich and cut it up into serving pieces.
- Chill the sandwiches before serving for 2 hours in the fridge.
- Enjoy.

Amount per serving (8 total)

Timing Information:

Preparation	
Cooking	40 m
Total Time	1 d 40 m

Nutritional Information:

Calories	987 kcal
Fat	62.8 g
Carbohydrates	63.2g
Protein	41.4 g
Cholesterol	97 mg
Sodium	3465 mg

* Percent Daily Values are based on a
2,000 calorie diet.

CREOLE PASTA II

Ingredients

- 6 tbsps butter
- 1 large onion, chopped
- 1 green bell pepper, chopped
- 3 stalks celery, chopped
- 1 clove garlic, minced
- 1 tbsp all-purpose flour
- 1 lb peeled crawfish tails
- 1 (8 oz.) package processed cheese food
- 1 C. half-and-half cream
- 2 tsps Cajun seasoning
- 1 pinch cayenne pepper, or to taste
- 1 lb dry fettuccine pasta
- 1/2 C. grated Parmesan cheese

Directions

- Fry the following in butter until soft: garlic, onions, celery, and bell pepper.
- Now add in your flour and stir for 9 mins.
- Add your crawfish and place a lid on the pan and lie the contents simmer for 17 mins.
- Combine the: cayenne, cheese, Cajun seasonings, and half and half.
- Set your oven to 350 degrees before doing anything else.
- Boil your pasta for 9 mins in water and salt. The remove all the liquid.
- Get a casserole dish and grease it with some butter. Then add your fish mix, and the noodles.
- Garnish everything with parmesan then cook the contents in the oven for 22 mins.
- Enjoy.

Amount per serving (8 total)

Timing Information:

Preparation	15 m
Cooking	1 h 15 m
Total Time	1 h 30 m

Nutritional Information:

Calories	490 kcal
Fat	22.6 g
Carbohydrates	48.9g
Protein	24 g
Cholesterol	122 mg
Sodium	682 mg

* Percent Daily Values are based on a 2,000 calorie diet.

Po' Boy

Ingredients

- Vegetable oil for deep-frying
- 4 French rolls, split and hinged
- 4 tbsps melted butter
- 1 tsp minced garlic
- 3 eggs, beaten
- 2 tbsps Creole seasoning
- 3/4 C. all-purpose flour
- 2 lbs jumbo shrimp, peeled and deveined
- 2 C. Kikkoman Panko Bread Crumbs
- 2 C. shredded lettuce
- Remoulade sauce:
- 1/2 C. mayonnaise
- 1 tbsp horseradish
- 1 tsp pickle relish
- 1 tsp minced garlic
- 1/2 tsp cayenne pepper
- 2 tbsps Kikkoman Ponzu Lime

Directions

- Coat your bread with garlic and butter before doing anything else.
- Coat your shrimp with flour and creole seasoning.
- Then dip it in some whisked eggs, and finally in panko.
- Now deep fry the shrimp in 360 degree hot oil.
- Now get a bowl and mix: ponzu lime, mayo, cayenne, relish, and minced garlic to together evenly.
- Coat your bread with a nice amount of this mix on each side.
- Then top the coated bread with your deep fried shrimp and some lettuce.
- Enjoy.

Amount per serving (4 total)

Timing Information:

Preparation	10 m
Cooking	1 h
Total Time	1 h 10 m

Nutritional Information:

Calories	1257 kcal
Fat	50 g
Carbohydrates	127.3g
Protein	73.2 g
Cholesterol	1526 mg
Sodium	12641 mg

* Percent Daily Values are based on a 2,000 calorie diet.

JAMBALAYA V

Ingredients

- 2 tbsps margarine or butter
- 1/4 C. chopped onion
- 1/3 C. chopped celery
- 1/4 C. chopped green pepper
- 1 (14.5 oz.) can diced tomatoes
- 1 1/2 C. chicken broth
- 2/3 C. long grain white rice
- 1 tsp dried basil
- 1/4 tsp garlic powder
- 1/4 tsp black pepper
- 1/4 tsp hot sauce
- 1 bay leaf
- 2/3 C. diced cooked chicken breast
- 2/3 C. cooked crumbled Italian sausage
- 2/3 C. peeled cooked shrimp

Directions

- Fry your green peppers, onions, and celery for 7 mins until tender. Then add broth, bay leaf, tomatoes, basil, house sauce, pepper, and garlic, and rice.
- Get this mix boiling and then lower the heat.
- Place a lid on the pot and let the rice cook for 22 mins.
- Now add your shrimp, chicken and sausage and let everything simmer for 4 more mins.
- Take out the bay leaf and then serve.
- Enjoy.

Amount per serving (4 total)

Timing Information:

Preparation	30 m
Cooking	30 m
Total Time	1 h

Nutritional Information:

Calories	369 kcal
Fat	16.6 g
Carbohydrates	31.5g
Protein	20.7 g
Cholesterol	78 mg
Sodium	704 mg

* Percent Daily Values are based on a 2,000 calorie diet.

BOURBON CHICKEN II

Ingredients

- 4 tbsps olive oil
- 3 lbs skinless, boneless chicken breast halves - cut into 1 inch pieces
- 1 C. water
- 1 C. packed light brown sugar
- 3/4 C. apple-grape-cherry juice
- 2/3 C. soy sauce
- 1/4 C. ketchup
- 1/4 C. peach-flavored bourbon liqueur (such as Southern Comfort (R))
- 2 tbsps apple cider vinegar
- 2 cloves garlic, minced
- 1 tbsp dried minced onion
- 3/4 tsp crushed red pepper flakes, or to taste
- 1/2 tsp ground ginger
- 1/4 C. apple-grape-cherry juice
- 2 tbsps cornstarch

Directions

- Fry your chicken in a Dutch oven for 10 mins constantly stirring. Then place the chicken aside.
- Now add to the pot: ginger, water, red pepper, brown sugar, dried onion, 3/4 C. of fruit cocktail juice, garlic, soy sauce, vinegar, ketchup, and bourbon.
- Get this mix boiling and then add the chicken back in.
- Once everything is boiling again set the heat to low and simmer the mix until everything is thick for 20 mins.
- Take out the chicken again and place it aside with slotted spoon.
- Combine 1/4 C. fruit cocktail juice and cornstarch and then mix it with the sauce.
- Get the sauce boiling again for about 2 mins.
- Then add the chicken back to the mix and heat it through.

- Enjoy with rice.

Amount per serving (8 total)

Timing Information:

Preparation	15 m
Cooking	45 m
Total Time	1 h

Nutritional Information:

Calories	417 kcal
Fat	10.9 g
Carbohydrates	36.7g
Protein	37.1 g
Cholesterol	97 mg
Sodium	1382 mg

* Percent Daily Values are based on a 2,000 calorie diet.

THANKS FOR READING! NOW LET'S TRY SOME SUSHI AND DUMP DINNERS....

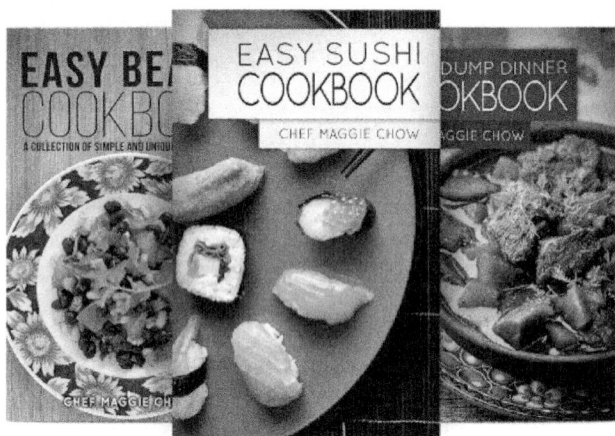

Send the Book!

To grab this **box set** simply follow the link mentioned above, or tap the book cover.

This will take you to a page where you can simply enter your email address and a PDF version of the **box set** will be emailed to you.

I hope you are ready for some serious cooking!

Send the Book!

You will also receive updates about all my new books when they are free.

Also don't forget to like and subscribe on the social networks. I love meeting my readers. Links to all my profiles are below so please click and connect :)

Facebook

Twitter

COME ON...
LET'S BE FRIENDS :)

I adore my readers and love connecting with them socially. Please follow the links below so we can connect on Facebook, Twitter, and Google+.

Facebook

Twitter

I also have a blog that I regularly update for my readers so check it out below.

My Blog

CAN I ASK A FAVOUR?

If you found this book interesting, or have otherwise found any benefit in it. Then may I ask that you post a review of it on Amazon? Nothing excites me more than new reviews, especially reviews which suggest new topics for writing. I do read all reviews and I always factor feedback into my newer works.

So if you are willing to take ten minutes to write what you sincerely thought about this book then please visit our Amazon page and post your opinions.

Again thank you!

INTERESTED IN OTHER EASY COOKBOOKS?

Everything is easy! Check out my Amazon Author page for more great cookbooks:

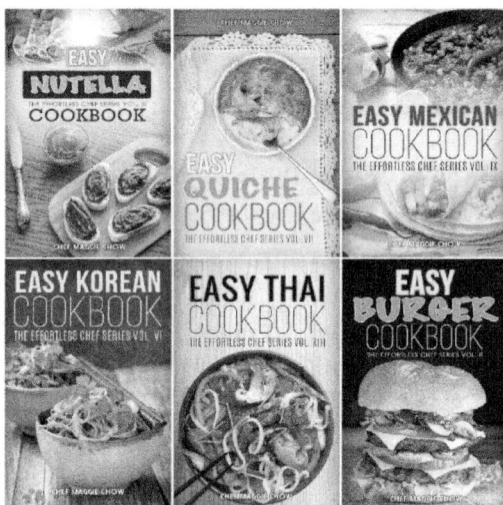

For a complete listing of all my books please see my author page.

Printed in Great Britain
by Amazon